SYNOPSIS

Obama's presidency has suffered the fiercest opposition any administration has had and yet Mr. Obama has managed to lead the country to financial reco-very, end the sen-seless war in Iraq, implement universal health-care, put an end to Iran's nu-clear ambitions and re-open diplomatic relations with Cuba all the while rema-ke US standing in the world. But if you ask his Repu-blican opponent, he is the worst pre-sident the country has had.
This book outlines the major accom-plishments of his presidency.

MIKE DUCHEINE

The OBAMA LEGACY

COPYRIGHTS

DEDICATION

This book is dedicated exclusively to my wife for her unrelenting support, her incredible patience, her unlimited understanding and her immeasurable and infinite love.

Preface

This book was written, edited and published entirely by Mike Ducheine; my objective is to provide some context into Obama presidency.

Mike Ducheine
twitter: @mducheiney
mducheiney@gmail.com

Since his inauguration in 2008, the president has not received any support from any Republican Legislator in Washington. This is unprecedented.

Although it is common practice that party affiliation determines the level of support (how much or how little) a president would receive from the Legislators of the opposing party, it is however extremely unusual that a sitting president would have so little cooperation from the Representatives of the opposing Party.

While it seems obvious by most analysis that the main factor is the president's race, it is worth noting that the President has also adopted a "non-mingling" approach vis-à-vis the GOP Lawmakers in Washington.

Be it by design or simply because of the environment the Republicans had created, the president style is also a factor in the final outcome of the relationship. it would not have mattered anyway; in fact, from the very beginning, the Republican Legislators drew a line in the sand; they were very forthcoming in their agenda, to deny the president a second term, hardly a good way to jumpstart a new relationship.

Everything Republicans in Washington have done was to challenge the president not just in political sense; they've questioned his citizenship, they've attacked his patriotism; they've questioned his motives, his love for the country. As such, anyone can easily conclude that Mr. Obama has held

the office of the presidency under
extremely challenging circumstances.

This book is an attempt to provide a
factual account of Obama' presidency by
discussing a few of his accomplishments.

Table of Contents

The Meaning of Obama

If you were to come from another planet and visit Earth between January 2009 and the year 2016 and the first broadcasting station you tune in to on your visit to planet Earth is Fox Opinion, - *known and referred to by most as Fox News* - the word Obama, the expression Barack Obama (and any derivation of the word) would have probably meant "complete failure", "utmost evil", "despicable organism" or simply "irritating parasite". According to Fox Opinion, Obama presidency has been a disaster, much, much worse than that of George W. Bush.

Seriously!

If there is anything remotely good or positive which happens under his administration, it must have been inevitable, something which would have happened anyway, irrespective of the occupant of the Oval Office. **In other words, according to Fox Opinion, if it's bad, Obama is responsible; if it's good,**

Obama cannot claim credit because it's probably a fluke, an anomaly. But Fox Opinion has failed short to point out that "Evil King Obama" has managed to seduce a whole nation, well, most of the nation (the world even) to accept him as commander-in-chief of the most powerful nation on earth, the United States of America, despite being a foreigner. God forbid! He may not even be a citizen. The GOP mouthpiece (Fox Opinion) may be on to something but a few details its hosts may have overlooked are discussed below in order to provide a more complete picture regarding the extent of the failure of the Obama's presidency.

Whenever an important issue such as terrorism arises, one is certain to hear many different views and opinions on how best to handle the aftermath of a tragedy such as the Brussels' airport attacks on March 22, 2016. The opinions are usually framed according to the Party the individuals belong to. In other words, you'd be hard pressed to hear any objective analysis of those types of situation. Each party wants to discuss those topics in such a way to score political points, especially in an election cycle such as the presidential elections we're in now, even if it means that the country would not benefit of their arguments. So, it should not surprise anyone to hear many different views, opinions and commentaries regarding not only the Brussel's terrorist attacks but also how president Obama handled or reacted to the tragedies.

That's where I come in. As I mentioned frequently in my blog (http://peoplebranch.org), I have no allegiance to any political party or candidate which frees me to be more or less objective in all matter politics. This is not to say one would agree with everything I write about; this is not to imply that I am 100% bias free. Far from it! I am still human, you know. However, because I am not in a race to please one party or the other, one candidate or another, one group or

another, I can be more objective than most.
Having said that, we will take a look at
how Republicans and Democrats have judged
Obama vis-à-vis his legacy in general and
the tragedies of terrorism in particular
which have thus far claimed the lives of
hundreds and injured thousands here and
abroad during his eight years in office. We
will also look at the devastation of
terrorist actions (here and abroad), their
aftermath and Obama's reactions through
three different prisms, the Republican's,
the Democrat's and the Objective's (which
is neither Republican nor Democrat). Let's
get to it.

The Republican Prism

*Obama is probably the worst president in
modern time; as the first black president,
Mr. Obama is a disgrace to the Black
community. Minority is worse off under
Obama than any other president in recent
memory. The country is worse off than when*

he took office; he implemented policies which do not align with American values; his immigration policy is the worst of all times, he has allowed 11 million illegal immigrants in the country; he made a deplorable nuclear deal agreement with Iran; he doesn't support our friend and ally Israel; he jeopardized freedom of religion; he has stifled freedom of speech. The country has lost respect overseas. Libya is now a mess; Syria is in shambles. All in all, Obama's presidency is much, much worse than George W. Bush. What you just read is an autopsy of the Obama administration by the Republican Party.

It is a very foggy prism to look through when it comes to Obama. **Since he's occupied the Oval Office, there is never a single word Mr. Obama has uttered or a single action he has taken or a single move he has made which is considered good by the Republicans.** You can understand the dilemma, can't you? Even if one were to be the most stupid individual on the planet, there are times when that "stupid individual" would do something or say something, even despite himself/herself, which would be good, let alone a Harvard graduate, an accomplished Senator, a calculated politician and now the president of the most powerful country on earth. You can appreciate the dilemma, can't you? If you tune in to any broadcaster/entertainer in the GOP camp (Sean Hannity and company at Fox, Rush Limbaugh (who doesn't know Rush?), Glenn Beck and the whole gang of Republican broadcasters, reporters, journalists, opinion writers, commentators, etc.), Obama's presidency has been a disaster. Even what appears to be good such as a low unemployment rate is attributed to something other than Obama's policy or actions his administration has taken to tackle the high unemployment problem he inherited when he took office. In other words, **Obama has not, does not and will not do anything which is right when looked through the Republican Prism.** It should not be any surprise to you (or anyone else) that his reactions in regards to the Airport tragedies in Brussels caused by terrorism were wrong. Printed everywhere Republican, he should have done this, he should have done that, he should have done the other. The Republican candidates vying for the Oval Office jumped on the bandwagon to give their two-cents opinion, and if you guessed that they think the president didn't react properly, you must be a psychic. John Kasich suggested he would have ended the current course of event, turned Air Force One around to come back to Washington. Hmm! Suffice to say that the president of the United States is always in office no matter where he's at. Coincidentally, Air Force One was built as a mobile office for the President of the United States. John Kasich of all people – *he was a politician in Washington* – should know that the President is abreast of any situation no matter where he is at in the world. So, the call to "turn Air Force One around" is at best cheap political shots. Well, I did say we were looking at Obama's

presidency through the Republican prism,
didn't I?

The Democrat Prism

Looking through the Democrat Prism is
somewhat less foggy albeit slightly biased,
understandably so; Democrats tend to be
more independently minded and very diverse
in their opinions in regards to their Party
in general and the president in particular.
Some Democrats believed the President
reacted appropriately in regards to the
Brussels Airport explosions, continuing
whatever course he was in; other Democrats
thought he should have handled the news of
the tragedy differently. As it might
already be obvious, Democrats are usually
more inclined to strike a balance, be it
about a Democratic or a Republican
President. As such, the president's
reactions to the terrorist actions in
Belgium were met with mixed reactions in
the Democrat camp. For instance, contrary

to Republicans who saw everything George W. Bush did – *including misleading the country about existence of weapon of mass destruction (WMD) in Iraq in order to take the country to war* - when he was in office as good but whatever Obama does as bad or wrong, both Tom Brokaw and Chris Matthews of MSNBC (a Democrat leaning network) lambasted Obama for "not acting like a leader". Tom Brokaw angrily uttered "Time to be the leader" and proceeded to recite a list of terrorist acts which have happened since September 11, 2001; Chris Matthews thinks that "Obama Off Base in response to Brussels' attacks, you don't want to hear he phoned it in". And of course there were many legislators and members of his cabinet who came out to his defense, rightfully so; that's their primary task, to support and defend their employer. This is not to imply that the diverse reactions by the Democrats vis-à-vis the president regarding the terrorist act at the Brussels' Airport (or any other similar situation) are correct or appropriate. Both criticism and support

could be off base, for the public does not
have the relevant information the President
of the United States uses to make
decisions. The example serves to outline
the contrast between Democrats and
Republicans in general.

Obama A Political Houdini

Some analysts are inclined to refer to
Barack Obama as a political Houdini. Harry
Houdini, an early 20th century magician, is
believed to have performed sensational
escape acts which has defied logic. Most of
his magic acts consisted having both his
hands and feet cuffed and chained
(sometimes in straight jacket) and dropped
under water. He would manage to free
himself and emerge above water unscathed.
His most daring act was to be buried alive,
leaving just enough room so he could claw
himself from the grave should he survive;
well, he did.

Without the entertainment aspect of the escape acts, Barack Obama has managed to put Harry Houdini to shame. While Harry Houdini's acts were believed to be staged (which most likely were), Obama has never had the luxury to perform illusory acts on his audience a) the recession was not fake and could not be staged when he took office b) the Wall Street fallout was not staged when he took office c) the auto industry in shambles was not staged when he took office d) the mounting deficit could not be staged when he took office e) the mounting debt was not fake when he took office f) the million dollar daily cost of the ongoing wars in Iraq & Afghanistan was not an act when he took office g) the high unemployment rate was not staged when he took office.

But the modern day political Houdini Barack Obama, with both hands and feet chained by the Republican led House and the Senate, managed to free himself and accomplished

what was perceived as impossible to do even without the restrictions.

Put differently, Barack Obama performed the greatest magic act never attempted by any politician on the planet, a daring escape not even Harry Houdini could have achieved.

The Objective Prism

Because human bias cannot be completely removed, most analysis would usually reflect that; however, if one is rational and genuinely wants to form an objective opinion about something or someone, it is still possible. We will attempt to submit opinions based almost exclusively on analysis of facts, events and circumstances; we will try as best as possible to avoid discussing our preferences or to even judge others'. Our primary objective is to let the facts do the talking.

On the historic day of the inauguration of Barack Obama as first black president of the United States, a few blocks away, the Republican elites, powerbrokers and legislators gathered, not to celebrate or even acknowledge history but to devise a plan on how best to make Obama's presidency a blip, an irrelevancy at best but a disastrous one nevertheless. The very next day, GOP Majority Leader Senator Mitch McConnell from Kentucky publicly outlined his most important agenda: to make Barack Obama a one-term president regardless the cost and the consequences (to the country and its citizens). Mitch wasn't joking; it wasn't politics as usual. His statement was crafted after a series of discussions overnight with GOP leaders and powerbrokers during the president's inauguration. Without re-hashing the Republican House performance during Obama's presidency, Mitch worked hard to make good on his promise. Rush Limbaugh – *a Republican idealist broadcaster/entertainer* – expressed in one sentence what the

Republican Legislators set out to do: "I hope the president fails".

Coincidentally, most Republican and Republican leaning individuals share Mitch's ideals; they all helped him along the way; in addition to creating the Birther Movement whose only purpose for existing was to delegitimize Obama as president, they insulted him regularly, they opposed everything he attempted to do to move the country forward. Rush Limbaugh – *a man who needs no introduction* – summed up the feeling of the Republicans (voters and leaders) at the time: I hope the president fails he said on his show shortly after Obama assumed the presidency. **Here is in essence what president Obama had to deal with during his presidency: a concerted effort to oppose everything he tries to do, an irrational call for him to fail.** It was the first time in the history of the presidency that a president did not have a single ally on any policy from the opposing party. Most Republicans are quick to dismiss the idea of the president's race factored in their extreme position. For over two hundred years, politics has always been bad, ugly, nasty even but history has never recorded such extreme position taken by the opposing party until Obama presidency. Is it just a coincidence that the first black president is treated just like any other black? Irrespective of what it is, Barack Obama has not only soared above the fray – *he took the high road* – but he has managed to get a lot done during his presidency despite all obstacles laid on his political path by the Republicans. Below, we discuss some of the most important items Obama had on his agenda when he took office and how he fares a few months away from leaving office.

FOREIGN POLICY

Republicans in general like to argue against facts in general, in reference to Obama in particular; as such, it should not surprise anyone to hear Republicans reflect that the country is in much worse shape today under Obama than it was under George W. Bush and U.S. standing in the world is at its lowest since Obama took office. Unsurprisingly, Fox Opinion – *known and referred to by most as Fox News* – bears a major portion of the blame. Most Republicans tune in almost exclusively to Fox' programs which support their ideals and beliefs, however facts free those programs are. To every host at Fox, Obama did not and could not possibly do anything good or right.

On Tuesday, June 2nd 2015, Gretchen Carlson, host at Fox said this:

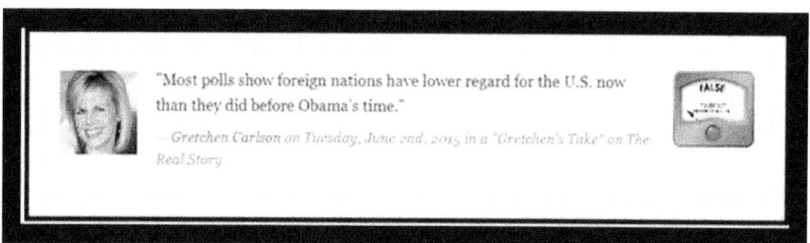

"Most polls show foreign nations have lower regard for the U.S. now than they did before Obama's time."

—Gretchen Carlson on Tuesday, June 2nd, 2015 in a "Gretchen's Take" on The Real Story

a statement that is <u>proven completely false</u> according to Politifact.com. US standing in the world during the Bush administration is best explained by then President of Venezuela, Hugo Chavez. In his speech at the United Nations in 2006, he referred to President Bush as "the devil" who thinks he is "the owner of the world."

"Yesterday, the devil came here. Right here. Right here. And it smells of sulfur still today, this table that I am now standing in front of." Mr. Chavez said to the General Assembly.

You don't need Politifact or any other facts check organization to know that U.S. standing in the world could not possibly be worse under Obama than it was under Bush. After alienating allies such as France, Spain, Italy, Germany, the Bush administration adopted an arrogant posture towards US allies even in the face of investigations which proved that the world was misled by his administration. Here at home, the verdict was swift and decisive; the election of Obama, a junior Senator with no foreign policy experience over John McCain, a war hero, a politician and an individual with foreign policy experience settled the matter that the electorate were not happy with Republican president in the Oval Office.

Contrary to George W. Bush, the Obama administration' approach to the world was conciliatory, to the point of being accused by the Republicans to be a weak president. His speech in Cairo, Egypt on June 4, 2009, just six months in his presidency, was an olive branch extended to the Muslim community, a major departure from the previous administration whose primary focus was to wage wars against the Muslims and beyond. Obama's attempt to reconcile US with the Muslim world created friction between the United States and the State of Israel, a conundrum his administration has been operating under and around for the major part of his presidency. A nuclear agreement with Iran - *a positive step to end Iran' nuclear ambitions by any analysis* - contributed to exacerbate the friction between US and Israel, the latter having publicly and adamantly opposed the agreement. The rest of the world community however saw those overtures by the Obama administration as the right approach. On the world stage, US has regained some level of prestige which was badly damaged during the Bush years. As shown in the graph below provided by Pew Research Center, European nations give US a higher approval "to do the right thing" rating (more than 20 points by Spain & Germany, more than 30 points by France and UK) under Obama than under the Bush administration.

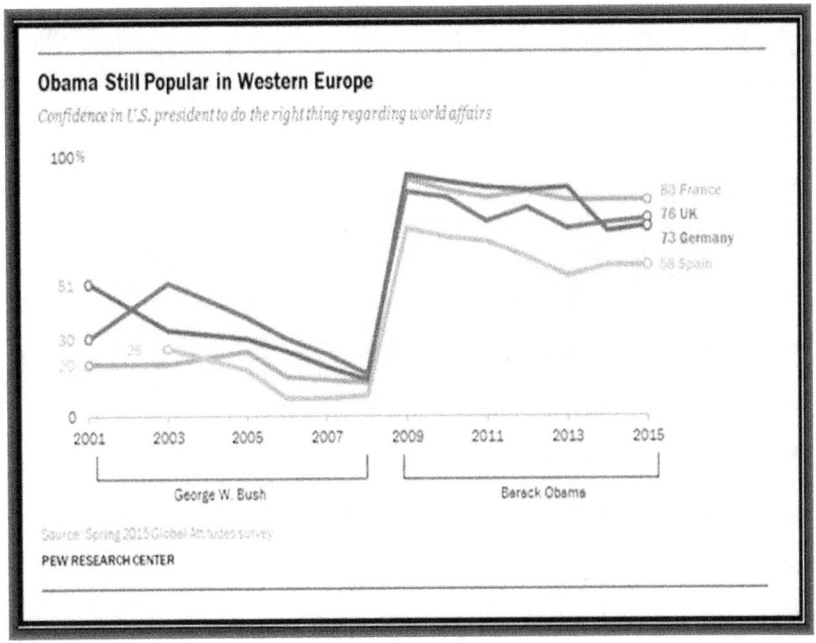

Obama Still Popular in Western Europe

Confidence in U.S. president to do the right thing regarding world affairs

- 83 France
- 76 UK
- 73 Germany
- 58 Spain

George W. Bush | Barack Obama

Source: Spring 2015 Global Attitudes survey

PEW RESEARCH CENTER

So, it is difficult if not impossible to imagine that US standing on the world stage is worse under Obama than it was under George W. Bush.

In a major reversal of US policy towards Cuba, Obama negotiated through diplomatic back-channels with Canada serving as intermediary the lifting of the embargo on Cuba. On March 21-22 2014, on the backdrop of Cuban exiled protests on the streets of Miami, Florida, Obama (and his family) took a trip to Havana, Cuba to meet with Raoul

Castro, the current president of Cuba and visit historic sites. And on August 31, 2016, the first US commercial flight in more than 50 years landed in Cuba. Obama also visited Argentina in a move to bury the hatchet between the two states; Argentinian were subjected to tortures and mass executions in the "dirty war" under dictator Pinochet who was initially supported by the US government. Obama's visit to Argentina was to allay the concerns of the Argentinians and reiterate US commitment to human rights; as a gesture of good faith towards the Argentinian people, Obama proposed to de-classify documents related to the periods of US relations with dictator Pinochet. Those overtures by the Obama administration have helped elevate US standing in the world. The chart below provides a glimpse how much US foreign policy has impacted the country standing in the world over the years.

U.S. Favorability	Under George W. Bush								Under Barack Obama						
	1999/2000	2002	2003	2004	2005	2006	2007	2008	2009	2010	2011	2012	2013	2014	2015
	%	%	%	%	%	%	%	%	%	%	%	%	%	%	%
Canada	–	72	63	–	59	–	55	–	68	–	–	–	64	–	68
France	62	62	42	37	43	39	39	42	75	73	75	69	64	75	73
Germany	78	60	45	38	42	37	30	31	64	63	62	52	53	51	50
Italy	76	70	60	–	–	–	53	–	–	–	–	74	76	78	63
Poland	86	79	–	–	62	–	61	68	67	74	70	69	67	73	74
Spain	50	–	38	–	41	23	34	33	58	61	64	58	62	60	65
UK	83	75	70	58	55	56	51	53	69	65	61	60	58	66	65
Russia	37	61	37	46	52	43	41	46	44	57	56	52	51	23	15
Ukraine	–	–	–	–	–	–	–	–	–	–	–	–	–	68	69
Turkey	52	30	15	30	23	12	9	12	14	17	10	15	21	19	29
Jordan	–	25	1	5	21	15	20	19	25	21	13	12	14	12	14
Lebanon	–	36	27	–	42	–	47	51	55	52	49	48	47	41	39
Palest. ter.	–	–	0	–	–	–	13	–	15	–	18	–	16	30	26
Israel	–	–	78	–	–	–	78	–	71	–	72	–	83	84	81
Australia	–	–	59	–	–	–	–	46	–	–	–	–	66	–	63
China	–	–	–	–	42	47	34	41	47	58	44	43	40	50	44
India	–	–	–	–	–	–	–	–	–	–	–	–	56	55	70
Indonesia	–	–	–	–	38	30	29	37	63	59	54	–	61	59	62
Japan	77	72	–	–	–	63	61	50	59	66	85	72	69	66	68
Malaysia	–	–	–	–	–	–	27	–	–	–	–	–	55	51	54
Pakistan	23	10	–	21	23	27	15	19	16	17	12	12	11	14	22
Philippines	–	90	–	–	–	–	–	–	–	–	–	–	85	92	92
South Korea	58	52	46	–	–	–	58	70	78	79	–	–	78	82	84
Vietnam	–	–	–	–	–	–	–	–	–	–	–	–	–	76	78
Argentina	50	34	–	–	–	–	16	22	38	42	–	–	41	36	43
Brazil	–	–	–	–	–	–	–	–	–	62	62	61	73	65	73
Chile	–	–	–	–	–	–	55	–	–	–	–	–	68	72	68
Mexico	68	64	–	–	–	–	56	47	69	56	52	56	66	63	66
Peru	74	67	–	–	–	–	61	–	–	–	–	–	53	65	70
Venezuela	–	–	–	–	–	–	–	–	–	–	–	–	53	62	51
Burkina Faso	–	–	–	–	–	–	–	–	–	–	–	–	–	–	79
Ethiopia	–	–	–	–	–	–	–	–	–	–	–	–	–	–	81
Ghana	–	83	–	–	–	80	–	–	–	–	–	83	77	89
Kenya	94	80	–	–	–	87	–	90	94	83	–	81	80	84
Nigeria	–	–	–	–	–	–	–	–	81	–	–	69	69	76
Senegal	–	–	–	–	–	–	–	–	–	–	–	81	74	80
South Africa	–	65	–	–	–	–	60	–	–	–	–	72	68	74
Tanzania	–	53	–	–	–	46	65	–	–	–	–	–	75	78
Uganda	–	74	–	–	–	84	–	–	–	–	–	73	62	78

Note: 1999/2000 survey trends provided by the U.S. Department of State.

Source: Spring 2015 Global Attitudes survey, Q12a.

The column on the left of the chart shows US Standing in the world under George W. Bush in his first year in office; as it is evident, Canada and most European countries held US in high esteem; US fares well above 50 in most countries including Latin American countries. After the Iraq war which occurred in 2003 under very suspicious circumstances created by the Bush administration, US standing in the world plummeted to well under 50 in most countries. As the world learned that it was an elaborate scheme by the Bush administration to go to war with Iraq, US standing on the world stage had continued to suffer and its rating continued to plummet. Distrust of everything the US government said was at an all-time high. The world simply didn't want to hear anything the US government had to say. When Obama assumes the presidency, he resets the world' view about US. His visited to Cairo, Egypt to re-assure the world of US commitment to work towards peace and diplomacy instead of the previous approach which resulted almost exclusively in waging war against any country (overwhelmingly Muslim) the US didn't consider as ally. As such, the reversal in US international policy approach has contributed greatly to a gradual increase in US standing on the world stage, except for a few Muslim countries (ironically) and Russia where US standing stays in the low ten.

UNEMPLOYMENT

When Obama took office in January 2009, the
US unemployment rate was at a national
average of 9.3%; 14 states (including
California, Florida, Illinois, North
Carolina and Florida) were even worst;
their unemployment rate was at a10% or
higher. The country was shedding jobs at an
average of 250,000 per month; according to
a report published on November 2008 - *just
two months prior to Obama assuming the
presidency* - by the Economic Policy
Institute (EPI), there were already over
ten million (10,000,000) people unemployed
in the country, and the projected monthly
unemployment estimates gave no reason to
smile either; the country would continue to
shed jobs in the next few months at the
same rate (or worse).

Ironically, Republican Legislators in
Washington were smiling. - *I did not make
that up* - Despite the fact that Obama

inherited the recession, they were very elated; they saw an opportunity to make good on Mitch's promise to make Obama a one-term president; they saw a silver lining for the Republican Party. To the detriment of the unemployed and at the cost of the country falling further into the recession, the GOP Representatives - *whose primary concern should have been to work with the president to revive the economy* - devised a strategy, not to help the president get people back to work but to reframe the discussion. The strategy was several fold a) to blame the president for not doing enough to get people back to work b) to constantly block whatever the president tried to do to remedy the situation c) to get the Republican constituents to believe that Obama created the problem. To everyone' surprise, the GOP Representatives' strategy worked, with some help from the Party mouthpiece of course, Fox Opinion, - *known and referred to by most as Fox News* - Rush Limbaugh, Ann Coulter et al.

In fact, polls taken Jan 21-25 2009 put the president at 41% job approval rating among Republicans; the polls were completely irrelevant and could not possibly have anything to do with the new president. Barack Obama was sworn in in January 20, 2009. Obviously, polls taken the next four days couldn't possibly provide any useful information as far as Obama's job approval rating, and yet, the GOP constituents couldn't bring themselves to even give the guy a chance to prove himself but by the end of 2009, Obama approval rating among Republicans was at 16% and had continued to slide down to single digit. The last poll per this writing (Jun 20-26 2016) placed the president at just 11% approval rating among Republicans. **Surely, GOP Representatives have done a fantastic job brainwashing the Republican constituents to dislike the president but there is one area they couldn't prevail, <u>in the facts</u>**. No matter how much GOP leaders hate Obama, they cannot change the facts. Today, the unemployment rate stands at just 4.7%

according to the Bureau of Labor Statistics
News Release on June 3, 2016.

Although the GOP Representatives (as well
as the constituents) have plenty to be
thankful about in regards to Obama's
leadership, they've continued to "dog him"
regarding the job market. **Republicans
Leaders cannot come to grip that despite
their nefarious and malicious attitude
towards the president and their constant
opposition towards him, he has prevailed.**

It is one thing to hate an individual but
it's mind boggling to gamble the fate of a
whole country in order to score political
points and yet still lose. That has to
sting. But what's even most mysterious is
the fact that the Republican constituents
are unable to set aside their hatred for
Obama to acknowledge they too have
benefited from his leadership in regards to
the job market. However, when GOP leaders
are asked whether they are patriots, they
find the question insulting but they had no
qualm pushing the country further into

recession in order to get rid of Obama. - *I do ponder sometimes whether Republican Leaders are deprived of a functioning brain. Has their hatred for Obama stripped them all of a rational mind? Or has their hatred blinded them?* - Below is a chart from the Bureau of Labor Statistics which provides a glimpse of the state of the job market (8+% unemployment rate) when Obama assumed the presidency in January 2009 and the state of the job market as of November 2015 (4.7% unemployment rate).

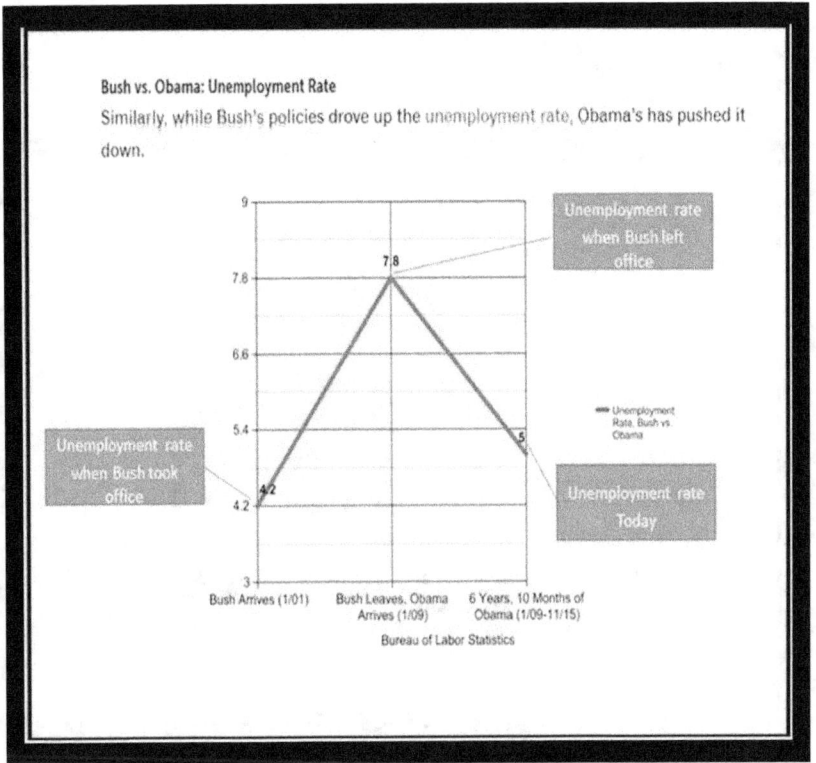

Bush vs. Obama: Unemployment Rate

Similarly, while Bush's policies drove up the unemployment rate, Obama's has pushed it down.

Bureau of Labor Statistics

As it should be obvious, when Obama took office on January 2009, the country was hemorrhaging jobs at a dizzying rate (462,000 in January 2009 alone). By November 2015 (last year), the Obama administration has recorded net private sector jobs created slightly under 13 million (13,000,000) as displayed in the chart below

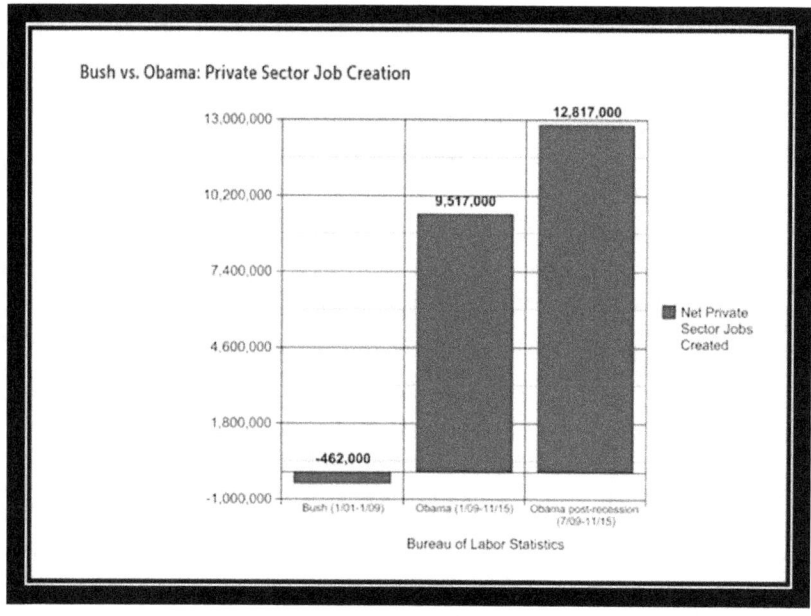

This information is available to anyone who cares to acquire them; they were provided by the same agency responsible to collect these types of information under every president. (Bureau of Labor Statistics)

It is mind boggling to grasp the justification any Republican leader who aspires to become president would have to deceive the constituents he wishes to lead someday; but it is even more troubling that the constituents are so gullible, so ignorant of the current state of affairs; it is troubling they have no idea what's going on in their own country. One doesn't have to like an athlete or a team to acknowledge his performance or superiority, do you agree? It seems as if the Republican Party in its entirety is under some sort of spell which deprives its members of the simplest form of "logical reasoning."

ECONOMY

When former Senator John Kerry, now serving as Secretary of State in Obama administration, bid for the office of the presidency in 2004, he used a famous line – *coincidentally which was and is still true* – in an attempt to appeal to the electorate, mostly Independents and Republicans whose focus and priority could be the economy, **"if you want to live like a Republican, you must elect a Democrat."** Although his call did not produce the intended result, to elect him as president of the United States, - *the country was mostly focused on security after the September 11, 2001 attacks on US Soil by bin Laden* - John Kerry made a good point which is indeed supported by statistics. For the past six decades, economic performance has been mostly under Democratic presidents; US News reported on October 2015 in an article that "four of the five presidents who have overseen the largest average economic expansions since World War II have been Democrats - John F. Kennedy, Lyndon B. Johnson, Bill Clinton and Jimmy Carter".

While it is common practice for any Republican aspirant to the presidency to promise better economic future for all, although history is yet to record much success under Republican presidency, **it is disingenuous, downright deceiving to suggest that the economy is worse under Obama than it was under Bush;** ironically and most troubling is the fact that the Republican constituents actually believe that. I must admit that I have given up trying to understand this phenomenon; the data are available, proofs some of which are current, tangible and yet the Republican Party as a whole believes just the opposite. It's a mystery which simply cannot be deciphered.

When Obama took office in 2009, the country was in a grim recession; in addition to the job market which was in free fall, the financial sector – *fondly referred to as Wall Street* - brought the country to its knees. Policies which were enacted under the previous administration gave green light to funds' managers to gamble people's savings, retirements and investments, and they gleefully obliged. The result was a complete financial meltdown in 2008. Obama took office in January 2009; six years into his presidency, not only has the economy recovered somewhat but also corporate profits have more than doubled (see the graph below). That doesn't mean everything is rosy; when has it ever been? However, there is no comparison between the Obama administration and the Bush's when it comes to the economy. See the graph below which shows how corporate profits have skyrocketed under the Obama administration.

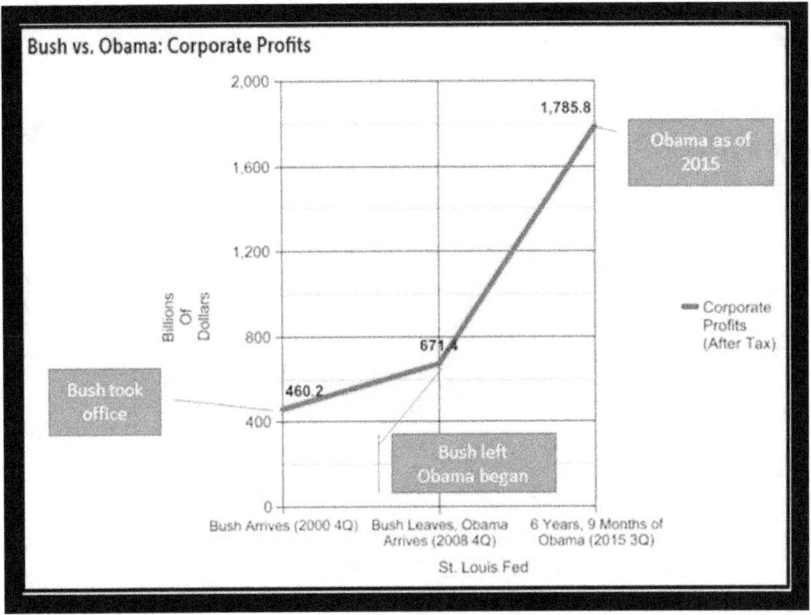

As illustrated in the graph above, when Bush exited the presidency, corporate profits were at approximately $671 billion; this was fantastic (for the corporate world of course) considering the rest of the country was struggling to go by but when Obama took office, corporate profits soared; by the third quarter of the year 2015, corporate profits were recorded at $1.8 trillion. So, how does one reconcile the argument that the Obama administration is against small businesses all the while

enacting policy and providing the platform
for such huge profits?

SPENDING

Remember the 2012 Obama bid for re-
election? Maybe not. But what you probably
remember is the famous 47% statement by
Mitt Romney? No? Well, that's okay. Let me
refresh your memory. In the 2012 bid for
the presidency, Mitt Romney, former
Governor of Massachusetts challenged Obama,
then incumbent to the presidency; the prize
was the Oval Office. The country was in the
worst economic state ever. After almost
three years in office, Obama was able to
slow down a bit the hemorrhage in the job
market but there were plenty of signs the
bleeding didn't stop; in fact, one could
say there was still internal bleeding.
There were plenty of signs everywhere that
the miracle the country expected from
Savior Obama didn't happen. To make
matters worse, the Republican led Congress
which had worked tirelessly to obstruct
everything Obama tried to achieve saw a

golden opportunity to help Mitch McConnell fulfill his congressional "duty" (the sacred goal he sets for himself on Obama's inauguration day) to make Obama a one-term president. Yes, you read correctly; to the detriment of the constituents (whether you're Democrat or Republican, you pay the same price, you suffer the same consequences), the Republican Congressmen did not only refuse to help Obama turn the economy around but they also stood on the way to prevent him from achieving anything for the country. **Republicans in Washington give patriotism a bad name.** Imagine for a moment that you are hired to do a job; you are provided no tool, no resource, no help. In addition, imagine that your employer also ties your hands, betting there will be plenty of opportunities to say you're not capable of doing the job; you are incompetent. Visualize that scenario for just a second. How could you do the job for which you would be hired? That was precisely the predicament Republican Representatives put Obama in; that was exactly what the Republicans in Washington expected to happen to the president, unable to do the job the American people entrust him to do. Interestingly, luckily or ironically, Obama had performed the most jaw-dropping magical act or the biggest political stunt in history, – *Even Harry Houdini would have had to learn a thing or two from Obama* – he has managed to perform the job (with both hands tied) for which he was hired better than even those whose hands were completely free, were provided all the tools and resources as well as assistance when needed.

According to the Congressional Budget Office (CBO), – *CBO is strictly nonpartisan; it conducts objective, impartial analysis; and hires its employees solely on the basis of professional competence without regard to political affiliation. CBO does not make policy recommendations, and each report and cost estimate summarizes the methodology underlying the analysis* – expenditures

under Obama have been flat, not only in
comparison to the Bush administration but
also in contrast to prophet Ronald Reagan.
The combined chart below gives an
interesting contrast between the Obama
administration and several previous
administrations.

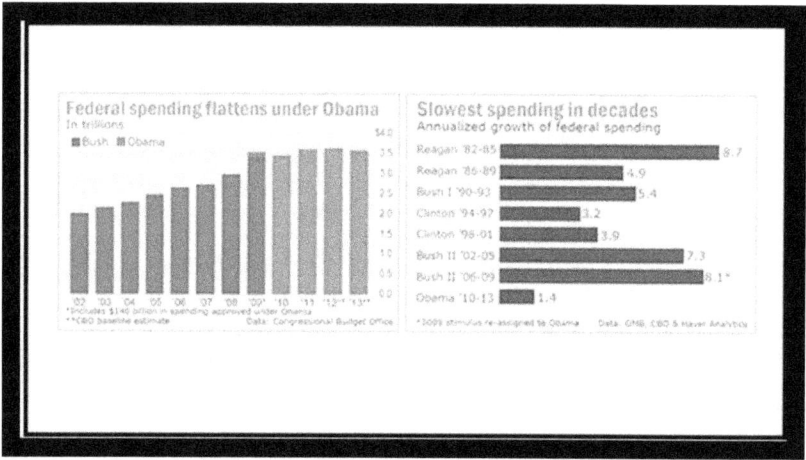

If you're not good in math, the graph above
should give you a pretty good understanding
of Obama' spending habit; even if you're
wearing your Republican glasses, it should
be obvious (even to a blind man) that there
are more expenditures which occur under
Republican administrations than under
Democrat's. For instance, under Ronald

Reagan, in his first term in office as president, federal spending was 8.7 percent; under Bush I, federal spending was 5.4 percent; under Bush II, federal spending was 7.3 percent. By contrast, under Bill Clinton, federal spending was 3.2 percent and under Obama in his first term, federal spending was just 1.4 percent. So, **if the Republican constituents were really, seriously concerned about government spending, they would have stopped voting for Republican legislators (and presidents) to represent them in Washington. <u>Otherwise, they should all stop the pretext that they care about government spending</u>**. As it stands today, according to FACTS, Republican administrations spend much, much more than Democratic administrations. When Bill Clinton left office in 2000, the country inherited a budget surplus of almost $2 trillion dollars ($1.9T). In his first year in office, George W. Bush wiped out the surplus. **Republicans should stop the**

pretext that they care about government spending; they don't.

It is also worth noting that the conclusion drawn by the Congressional Budget Office was shared by the Bureau of Economic Analysis (BEA) - *Source of US economic statistics including national income and product accounts (NIPAs), gross domestic product ... The BEA Advisory Committee advises the Director of BEA on matters related to the development and improvement of BEA's national, regional, industry, and international economic accounts, especially in areas of new and rapidly growing economic activities arising from innovative and advancing technologies, and provides recommendations from the perspectives of the economics profession, business, and government.* - The chart below shows a contrast in spending between the Reagan administration and the Obama's.

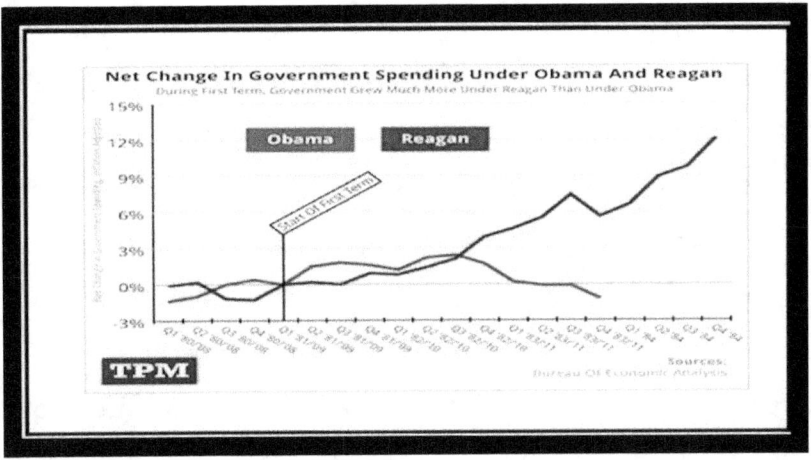

As it should be quite obvious by now,
Republican Legislators' outrage over Obama'
alleged outlandish spending is unwarranted,
theatrical and spreading rumors to this
regard is outright deception. Republican
Legislators make it their mission to argue
with facts, distort them and offer their
electorate a picture of the state of the
government which only exists in their
narrative; also unfortunately, the
Republican electorate have always chosen
the "facts free" reality which might
contribute to making Washington what it's
always been, a place where nothing is done.

Either the Republicans are confused between reality and wish or they simply don't care. The chart above – *provided by the Bureau of Economic Analysis* – shows both the Obama and the Reagan administration at the start of their respective first terms in office (look where it says START OF FIRT TERM). As you can see, at the end of Reagan's first term in 1984, spending has gone way up; by contrast, at the end of Obama's third year in his first term, spending fell below zero (0); yes, you read correctly, below zero. It did go slightly up to 1.4% the following year (2012).

DEBT

One of the most frequently used tool by candidates vying for the Oval Office is National Debt. Republicans are usually most successful in their marketing, not because they are right but rather because they're smarter than Democrats. If you've been paying very close attention, you'd notice that Republicans always bring the topic for discussion - *during campaigns and debates* - when a Democrat president occupies the White House but shy away from it when the occupant of the Oval Office is a Republican. The reason is actually a very simple one, - *as illustrated by the chart below* - **national debt rises drastically under Republican administrations**. No, this is not a typo, you read correctly.

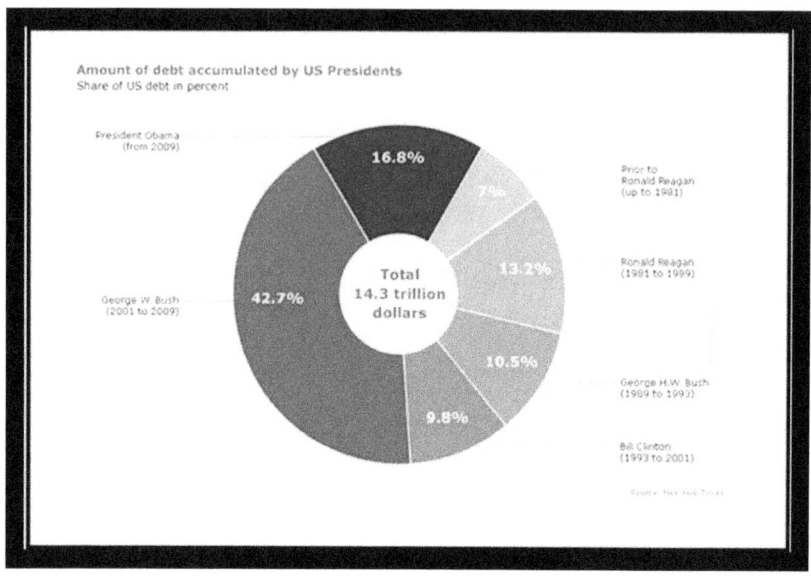

Amount of debt accumulated by US Presidents
Share of US debt in percent

President Obama (from 2009) — 16.8%

Prior to Ronald Reagan (up to 1981) — 7%

Ronald Reagan (1981 to 1989) — 13.2%

George W. Bush (2001 to 2009) — 42.7%

Total 14.3 trillion dollars

George H.W. Bush (1989 to 1993) — 10.5%

Bill Clinton (1993 to 2001) — 9.8%

Source: New York Times

As illustrated in the chart, under George W. Bush, the debt rose to 42.7%; actually, it was much worse than the number itself. George W. Bush inherited a budget surplus of almost $2 trillion dollars when he assumed the presidency.

The reason you may not know that is because 1) as mentioned previously, Republicans are mum when they're in control of the political machines in Washington 2) they raise the issue when Democrats are in control, thus giving you the impression that Democrats are irresponsible when it comes to national debt 3) Democrats are not comfortable using simple slogans to explain such a complex issue.

In fact, it is true that national debt is not a topic which can be discussed using a slogan or even in a presidential debate where only a few minutes are allocated for the discussion. Since Republicans have no qualm scaring the b-Jesus out of everyone and they're more concerned about scoring political points, they make use of any tool that's available. In addition, it's worth mentioning that Republicans don't care an iota about national debt. How could I possibly know that? If indeed they were a) the issue would not have been buried when they're in control, in a position to actually do something about it b) they would not have contributed to increase it – *at times drastically* – when they're in control.

So, it is logical to conclude the only reason they bring it up when they're not in control is to scare the electorate, deceive them and give them a reason NOT to vote for Democrats. The chart above which clearly show the contrast between Republicans and Democrats in terms of spending habit was provided by the New York times; one could argue about its accuracy; it could be wrong; it could be biased.

However, the chart below was provided by the Treasury Department

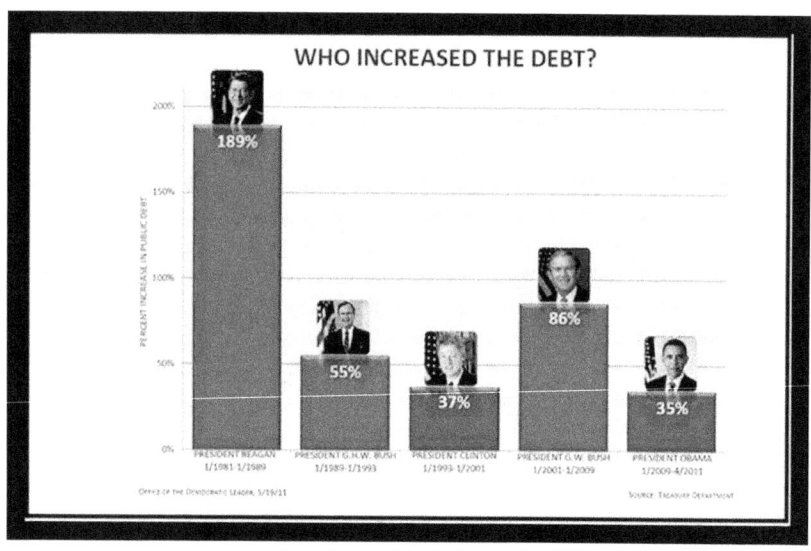

Fig 2

The graph above (Fig 2) reflects Obama administration up to April 2011, more than a year before the expiration of his first term in office; the graph below (Fig 3) provides a more comprehensive view of the spending habits of past presidents up to the end of Obama administration first term. Fig 3 displays how much is spent by each administration at the end of their respective first terms in office.

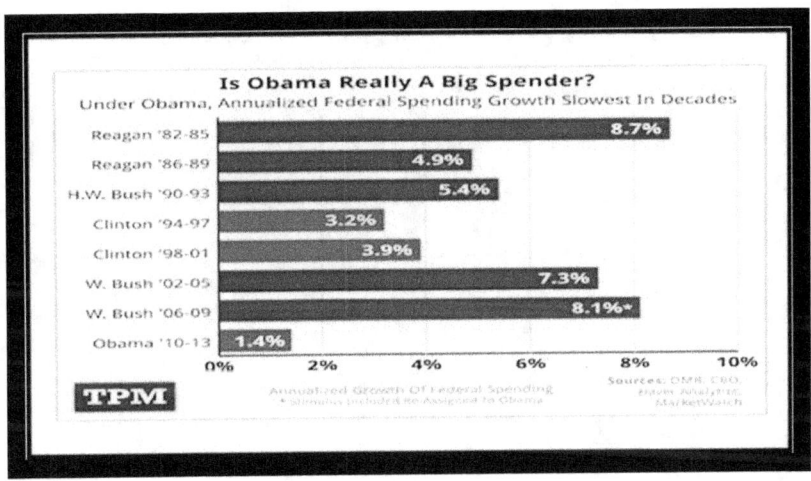

Fig 3

These data were provided by the Office of Management and Budget (OMB) supported by the Congressional Budget Office (CBO), both of which are independent agencies which operate under both major (or all) political Parties.

As mentioned earlier, the national debt is a very complex issue; although it is factually correct that Obama administration's debt is in par with other previous administrations, meaning no better no worse, - *except George W. Bush whose debt in his first term in office almost tripled the average of several previous administrations combined, as seen in the chart above.* - Republicans have always mixed various components of the debt in the debate to confuse the public, and they really want to confuse the electorate; it works to their advantage politically. National Debt in general should be discussed in conjunction with the Gross Domestic Product (GDP) which is calculated as follows:

GDP = C + G + I + NX

C is equal to all private consumption, or consumer spending, in a nation's economy, G is the sum of government spending, I is the sum of all the country's investment, including businesses capital expenditures and NX is the nation's total net exports, calculated as total exports minus total imports (NX = Exports - Imports). Without bogging you down with the intricate details in the calculation of the GDP and its correlation with the national debt, the presence of government spending (G) factor in the GDP calculation should trigger the flag of national debt changes.

SOCIAL ISSUES

Be it by coincidence or deliberate, Obama
will probably be known historically as the
President of the Firsts. He is already
(recognized as) the first black President
since the creation of the Republic. And
when it comes to social issues, Obama has
done everything possible to be the first to
tackle issues most administration would not
even consider let alone make a priority.

He is the first president who has
successfully implemented universal
healthcare (well, a version of it), not
without problems however. Even as of this
writing, a Damocles sword stills hangs over
the fate of Obamacare. The Republican led
Congress voted over 54 times to repeal the
Act, and if Donald Trump were to become
president, he promised to shred Obamacare
on Day one. Having said that, Mr. Obama is
nevertheless the first president who has

successfully implemented Universal
Healthcare for all.

Dancing with the Sexes

Obama is also fondly referred to as the
first LGBT president. No, he is not gay.
His relentless fight for minority rights
has also factored Lesbians Gay Bi-Sexual
and Transgender who have spent a great deal
of their lives hiding their true sexual
inclinations and gender identity.

The issue of homosexuals' rights has been
debated for decades here in the United
States. Bill Clinton, 42nd president, signed
an executive order (don't ask don't tell)
to shield anyone (in the Armed Forces) who
didn't specifically reveal their sexual

orientation from any punishment but it was Obama who has not only ended the practice of discrimination against homosexuals serving in the Armed Forces (by repealing "don't ask don't tell") but also signed an executive LGBT non-discrimination order "barring discrimination on the basis of sexual orientation or gender identity among federal contractors. The order also protects all federal employees from discrimination on the basis of gender identity" as reported on the July 21, 2014 article in Slate.com.

In order to circumvent Bill Clinton "don't ask don't tell" order, a number of States had moved to ban same-sex marriage; at the end of Bill's presidency in 2000, 31 states had passed law to ban same sex marriage. The number of states banning same sex marriage had continued to increase gradually as George W. Bush assumed the presidency in 2001. Interestingly in 2003, the state of Massachusetts - the first to have done so - passed law to legalize same sex marriage. Five years later in 2008, the state of Connecticut followed suit. When Obama assumed the presidency in 2009, it would be just a matter of time before same sex marriage becomes legal.

Even before the US Supreme Court ruled that the US Constitution guarantees the right for same-sex couples to marry in all 50 US states on June 26, 2015, a number of States had already opened their doors to same sex marriage, giving all married couples (heterosexual and homosexual alike) the same rights, benefits and privileges that were original reserved to heterosexual couples only. While there are still many states – *overwhelmingly Republican* – that have continued to resist the Supreme Court ruling, public pressure has forced government officials of those states (Governors, Senators) from passing laws or implementing policies which could have singled out homosexuals and penalized them. For instance, in North Carolina, a boycott on various business activities (entertainment, travel, shopping) by visitors and residents alike have made it impossible to enforce the law which would have forced transgender to use the bathroom which identifies with their physical sexual organs. Even law enforcement officers have backed out of trying to enforce the Governor's order.

Tangling With Prisoners

President Obama at the El Reno Prison Facility conversing with Four Prisoners

Since the creation of the Republic, no
sitting president has ever visited a
prison, Obama is the first. On July 2015,
the president of the United States made a
visit to a federal prison. I can only
imagine the level of scrutiny that facility
must have undergone by Secret Service and
the level of security which had to be in
place before the president's visit; after
all, it is an environment where even some
criminals fear for their lives. Regardless,
Obama toured the El Reno prison in Oklahoma
City; he sat down with half a dozen
inmates, the luckiest criminals on the
planet, at the very least in the United
States. The president brought attention to
the fact that the prison population has
more than quadrupled since 1980; Mr. Obama
called for reforms in the criminal justice
system in which non-violent criminals are
not locked up for the rest of their lives
behind bars. Mr. Obama stated that those
individuals need to be rehabilitated, not
incarcerated. Mr. Obama noted that it is in
the best interest of the States and of the

country to rehabilitate those individuals
(the non-violent criminals); the president
added that in addition to decreasing the
prison population, such approach would also
reduce the amount of money the government
has to spend to sustain those facilities. –
*At an average of $60 per day for each
prisoner, it costs the State almost $22,000
($21,900) per prisoner per year;
rehabilitation for the same prisoner would
have cost the taxpayers less than $10,000 -*

The president met with non-violent drug
offenders who are sentenced to die behind
bars; in an effort to jump start the
process of changes to the criminal justice
system, he commuted the sentence of 46
inmates and proposed to continue doing so
till the end of his second term in office.
As of June 2016, the president had commuted
the sentences of well over 340 prisoners
and as of August 2016, he has shortened the
sentences of more than 200 prisoners. Obama
reflected during his visit that, as a black

man in America, he could have wound up in jail.

The president's visit marks an important time in history; it outlines how deeply embedded racism has been in American culture. A study by major universities and independent organizations have shown there are as many Whites who have used drugs as there are Blacks and yet the prison population is overwhelmingly filled with minority offenders. 100+ years after the abolition of slavery, Blacks are still shackled; they are still discriminated against; they are still denied a good education; they are still denied a good job; they are still denied a promotion; they are still at the bottom of the financial ladder. They are still denied equal treatment in the justice system.

It is hopeful that the **Obama's visit to a prison and the announcement by the Department of Justice to transfer the management of the prison facilities to the States will help decrease the injustice**

towards the Black community in particular.
If nothing else, Obama opened the door for a more equitable justice system. It remains to be seen how much his effort is strengthened by future administrations.

SECURITY & TERRORISM

Whenever the topic of terrorism & security
arises, most Republicans are always quick
to suggest there was no act of terrorism in
the United States until Obama assumes the
presidency; some (mostly hosts and guests
on Fox Opinion including Mr. Giuliani of
all people, former mayor of NY who was in
office when the tragedy occurred)
overlooked that the tragedy of 9/11/2001
occurred under the Bush administration.
There are even jokes which suggest that
Obama is somewhat responsible for 9/11/2001
anyway, just for being Obama.

Notwithstanding the fact that 9/11 could have been avoided – *according to many sources at the Central Intelligence Agency (CIA)* - and there were plenty of acts of terrorism in US during the Bush administration (read details on politifact, dailykos, mediamatters, etc.), the most important point is ignored in the partisan-driven arguments; both Bush (after 9/11) and Obama had managed to keep major terrorist tragedies from being inflicted on the homeland. However, regardless the measure taken by those whose job is to protect the country, one must recognize there is **no system of security which can prevent individual acts of terrorism from happening 100% of the time, especially here in the United States where anyone can acquire a machine gun even on the internet.** No president can claim to be able to prevent individual and isolated cases of terrorism regardless of the security strategy in place.

So the argument – *in regards to domestic acts of terrorism which have occurred during Obama's presidency* - is at best misleading considering the drastic increase in firearm purchases since Obama has assumed the presidency. Domestic terrorism aside, the Obama administration has done in its second year in office what the Bush administration couldn't accomplish in eight years; he dedicated enough resources and made it a priority to find and kill Osama bin Laden, the individual who is believed to have been responsible for the worst terrorist attacks on US soil, the 9/11/2001 attacks.

Before Obama, the electorate were more inclined to elect a Republican candidate as president of the United States, especially when matters of security were at stake; Republicans were considered more effective than Democrats regarding external threats to US. Obama has completely changed the political landscape when it comes to ensuring the security of the homeland.

Having killed the believed mastermind behind the 9/11 attacks and having pursued a relentless campaign against leaders of terrorist groups across the globe, Obama has chipped away, considerably, the idea that a Republican is needed in the White House when the security of the country is at stake. The perception has completely evaporated with Obama's aggressive campaign to protect the homeland. Republicans can no longer claim monopoly in the security of the country, and it shows. Even during the 2016 presidential campaigns, the advantage Republicans usually enjoy - *by simply mentioning their strength to protect the country* - is virtually non-existent. They had good reason not to bring it up; Democrats would quickly remind them it was Obama who took care of the most notorious criminal, Osama bin Laden, something the Bush administration could not accomplish.

Brussels Airport Attack Aftermath

Having lost the argument in regards to the security and safety of the homeland, the Republicans have moved the pole again; the debate is no longer a national issue. Republicans have now resorted to terrorism overseas as a way to downplay and question the president's effectiveness vis-à-vis terrorism and security. They blamed the president for the Paris attack; they blamed the president for the Belgium attack; they continue to blame the president for all acts of terrorism which occurred outside the United States. Interestingly, dozens of terrorist attempts here in the United States have been foiled due to Obama's aggressive policy on stamping out terrorism. Besides, there were well over a dozen terrorist attacks on US interests overseas during the Bush administration. Contrary to Republicans however, Democrats have always considered those situations as scenarios the country has to deal with regularly, as cost of having a presence across the World.

Obama has made the safety of the homeland a very high priority in his administration, and it shows. Since he's been in the Oval Office, there's been zero successful large and elaborate terrorist attack on US Soil.

ENERGY & CLIMATE CHANGE

From Ronald Reagan to George W. Bush, the issue of Climate Change was reduced to a political ping pong match. Although each one of the administrations preceding Obama implemented some sort of policy to deal with this global threat, none of his predecessors took the issue seriously enough. In fact, the Bush (George W. Bush) administration refused to implement the Kyoto Protocol, - *an international treaty signed in 1997 in Kyoto, Japan that would require nations to reduce their greenhouse gas emissions* - citing economic setbacks (providing no specifics as to what those setbacks were) in the United States. But in February 2002, President George W. Bush set a voluntary "greenhouse gas intensity" target for the nation to encourage companies to voluntarily report and reduce their greenhouse gas emissions…"

The "voluntary target" set by the Bush administration was simply window dressing; in the United States, corporate social responsibility is at an all-time low; from Ronald Reagan to Obama today, the number of corporate scandals involving executives at the highest level of the organizations have not abated; every so often, major impact to the country has forced legislators in Washington to step in to rein in on corporate behavior.

As of the revision of this book, there is an ongoing hearing in Washington regarding Wells Fargo bad business practice towards the consumers, the gist of which consists in Wells Fargo's executives opening some two million accounts for their clients without their consent and knowledge; the practice contributed to padding the financial success of Wells Fargo, thus the ability to justify paying the executives responsible for such "genius marketing" over $100 million dollars in salary and bonuses all the while eliminating the jobs of well over 5,200 employees.

So, it is no consolation that the Bush administration sets a "voluntary" greenhouse gas emissions target for businesses. Republicans have always denied that climate change happens; in order to satisfy the Republicans and not anger the scientific community, the Bush administration left it up to the companies which could impact the environment to work towards reaching the "voluntary" target. As you might already guess, there is no penalty if those companies do not even try.

What is climate change? Weather is not climate change; most Republicans who have opposed any effort to curb global warming use the fact that it is cold during winter and it snows as proof that global warming is a hoax. The NASA website provides useful information regarding the two (weather and climate change) and explains the details of what climate change means to the world and how it would continue to affect the weather; you can read about it here.

It wasn't until Obama assumed office in 2009 that the issue of global warming/climate change took center stage along with healthcare. Barack Obama proves to be a different president when it comes to the issue; he doesn't simply talk about it; he works in collaboration with the world leaders to save the planet. So, in December 12, 2015, with US leadership, representatives (heads of states, scientists) of 195 nations gathered in Paris, France and signed an accord for the first time committing to lowering planet-warming greenhouse gas emissions, an effort they all agreed will help curb (or eliminate) the most drastic effects of climate change.

While the wing of the Republican Party has been playing footsie with the millions of lives here in the United States and billions across the world which would inevitably be impacted by such disaster, Obama has done what future generations – *including the very Republicans (who have opposed him throughout his presidency) and their offspring* – will be thankful for. The New York Time magazine penned an article in 2013 labeling Obama the Environmental President.

In addition to a sustaining campaign to combat climate change which threatens our planet, the Obama administration has also dedicated considerable resources to implement his energy plan which encompasses various elements: oil, wind energy, solar power, etc. and of course climate change.

In the 2008 presidential campaigns, there was an "uprising" against the idea of limited offshore drilling, the gist of which is the implementation of an energy policy which does not rely solely

on oil drilling and production but also
includes wind energy and solar power.

Then candidate Obama ran on the platform
to follow through with his plan to
implement comprehensive energy

policy if elected president but his
Republican challenger, John McCain
countered with "drill baby drill", a
complete repudiation of Obama energy plan.

During his presidency, Obama has not only
acted on the promise he made (in regards to
energy policy) but he has also raised fuel
efficiency standards for cars and trucks to
combat climate change; his Clean Power plan
also helps cut carbon dioxide emissions
from power plants.

Politics aside, "Obama had done more for
Clean Energy than you think" according to a
September 2015 article in the "Scientific
American" magazine.

It is difficult to assess whether Republicans' argument against Obama's energy policy has any merit; after all, Republicans are always against everything Obama. Regardless, Obama understands that damage to our planet is not a Democrat issue; it should concern every American citizen who wants to preserve the planet for future generations.

It is near impossible to comprehend why any individual (or group) would go against a policy that would benefit mankind. Be it hatred for Obama or complete ignorance, the outcome for the country, for the world is the same when the impact of climate change begins to exacerbate. Americans do not have the luxury of supporting their respective political Party on issues such as climate change which does not discriminate on the basis of political party; the future of our planet depends on everyone' collaboration and cooperation.

HEALTHCARE

During his campaign in 2008 for the
presidency of the United States, Obama
promised to reform the healthcare system;
his goal was to have everyone in America
covered under some sort of universal
healthcare system, much like Canada,
European countries or any developed
country; that was one of the few items in
then candidate Obama's check list if
elected president. Having defeated Senator
John McCain in the general elections, Mr.
Obama was sworn into office in January
2009. Upon assuming the presidency, Mr.
Obama made good on his campaign promise in
regards to the healthcare system; he sent a
comprehensive proposal to Congress, known
as the Patient Protection and Affordable
Care Act (PPACA) but widely known and
referred to (initially by foes) as
Obamacare. Both Houses (then led by
Democrats) gave green light to the
President's Healthcare policy – *It is worth
noting that NOT a single Republican voted*

for Obamacare - and On March 23, 2010,
President Barack Obama signed the act into
law.

In a logical
world where most
people could make
use of their
brains to parse,
dissect and
analyze

information, Obamacare would be considered
God sent for the nation but as you are
most likely aware, the Republican
constituents, led by their leaders in
Washington (the Representatives) and
Powerbrokers across the nation, organized
protests, spread rumors (about the act),
propagated false information (about its
impact on seniors: individuals advanced in
age) and used scare tactics to mobilize all
Republicans to oppose the act. Sarah Palin,
John McCain's running mate in 2008, -
famous for being able to see Russia from

her living room in Alaska; she was also the former Governor of the state of Alaska – spread the rumors that Obamacare would make use of a "Death Panel" for Seniors, the gist of which suggests that if you're a Senior and are not in good health, a panel of doctors would decide on whether you are treated back to good health or are put to death. Any rational individual would debunk that as nonsense; however, aided by its mouthpiece Fox Opinion – *known and referred to by most as Fox News* – and many other Republican broadcasting outlets (Limbaugh, Hewitt, etc.), the rumor took a life on its own and "Death Panel" was debated in every Republican circle as if it was true. **The Republican Party did a big disservice to its constituents; it misinformed them, it deceived them, it dragged them to protest against a policy which benefit them greatly** and thus made it extremely difficult (if not impossible) to improve and expand it.

Added to such fierce opposition of Obamacare by all Republicans, it didn't help Obama's cause that the website designed to accept registration into the program was not fully operational by the time the window for enrollment was opened. Such fiasco added fuel to the rhetoric by the Republicans that the Obamacare program would also be a fiasco. - *It should be noted that president Obama did indeed drop the ball; it is difficult to understand that a policy which could define his legacy was left so vulnerable to those types of problems. Obama should have been more pro-active; he should have been more hands-on -* In addition to promoting the (false) premise that Obamacare would cost jobs to hundreds of thousands (if not millions) of people, the technical glitches on the enrollment site were used as example by Obamacare's opponents that if a simple task such as enrolling people into the program is met with so many difficulties, one could only imagine how much more difficult it would be for the participants to obtain healthcare treatment after enrollment. - *That was fair criticism; Obama should have*

known better. He should have been
available, holding the hand of the
individual responsible to get the site
ready for enrollment; Obama did drop the
ball - Republicans capitalized on a problem
that mostly every new program would go
through regardless of the party which
introduces it; amidst the constant
opposition by Republican legislators who
want to ensure that Obamacare would indeed
be a failure, many Republican false
prophets rose up to predict that the worst
(about Obamacare) is coming; here is in a
nutshell what they were saying:

John Boehner, 1/6/2011: "When you step back
and look at the totality of this, I don't
think it's ever going to work."

John Boehner, 7/15/2012: "ObamaCare is only
making our economy worse, driving up health
costs and making it harder for small
businesses to hire."

**Victor Davis Hanson, National Review,
11/13/2013:** "In the next 90 days, the Obama

administration will have to declare victory and then abandon most of Obamacare. The legislation defies the laws of physics."

Bill Kristol, 11/3/2013: "Obamacare is failing and will fail. And I'm very much looking forward to being on this show [Meet the Press] with [David Axelrod] in January of 2017 when finally, all of Obamacare is repealed."

Rep. Paul Broun, 10/07/2013: "America is going to be destroyed by Obamacare, so whatever deal is put together must at least reschedule the implementation of Obamacare. This law is going to destroy America and everything in America, and we need to stop it."

Glenn Beck, 11/19/2009: "This is the end of prosperity in America forever, if this passes. This is the end of America as you know it."

Tom Coburn, 10/13/2010: "There will be no insurance industry left in three years. That is by design. You're going to make insurance unaffordable for everyone — which is what they want. Because if there's no private insurance left, what's left? Government-centered, government-run, single-payer health care."

Rush Limbaugh, 2/6/2014: "This is horrible for our country ... an absolute tragedy ... It breaks my heart folks to see this literal tragedy happen to this country ... Obamacare is going to cost this country two and half million jobs minimum."

Rand Paul, 2/20/2015: "I think that what's going to come out of ObamaCare is worse than anybody can imagine. I think it will lead to bankruptcy in the states that are fully embracing it."

Scott Walker, 2/20/2015: "In a 2013 interview with CNBC's Larry Kudlow, Wisconsin Governor Scott Walker argued that Obamacare was hampering the economic recovery."

<u>AND THEY WERE ALL WRONG</u>!

www.ingramcontent.com/pod-product-compliance
Lightning Source LLC
Chambersburg PA
CBHW060155290526
45789CB00003B/1052